# The
# Delicious
## Little Book
## of
## Love
## Laughter
## and Tears

by Stanley Kavan

# Dedication

*To a Great Lady*
*My Bride, Etta*

## Acknowledgement

With special thanks to collaborator, Amy Duggan, for her helpful editorial and graphic guidance in the preparation of this book.

# Overture

Ever since my grammer years, I've been enamored of poetry.
Poetry is the music of words…a correlation not original but apt.
And like music, it can be light or heavy, glad or sad, and transparent
or complex.

I've been especially fond of the traditional rhyming form with the
dynamics of cadenced words and phrases. Prose or free verse is
fine, too, but traditional verse has a grander invitation. It is more
melodious, more approachable for the reader and listener. And it is
a more challenging venue, the basic reason, in my belief, why it has
fallen out of favor in today's penchant for instant gratification. But
with its unlimited word choice, free verse does become the superior,
preferred medium for those ideas which require creative expanse,
ideas which otherwise, would be decidedly constrained by traditional
poetry's confined flexibility.

I'm also been intrigued with how a poems comes about. I find that as
interesting as the poem itself. I've never sat down and simply decided
to write a poem. Nor do most people who do creative writing. An
idea surfaces anywhere,anytime…driving, shopping, watching TV
or dropping off to sleep (the worst kind of moment) etc. It is carried
around in your craw sometimes for days, even weeks with words
forming and floating like jigsaw pieces waiting for eventual, formal
assembly. Often the idea takes on an unintended direction hardly
resembling its onset. Forks appear in the path, making a choice can
become…yes, exciting. Who would have thought that that emotion
could apply  to writing poetry? But it does.

Enough. Each of the poems that follow is preceded  by its story of
origin—that spark, that incendiary moment that led to its creation.
Do enjoy.

Stanley Kavan

# Contents

Sing Me!

Following the explanatory overture, this is kind of an opening curtain for the pieces to follow. Originally, it was written to inspire and accelerate entries for a poetry competition I chaired ... ergo, "calling all poets" as the subtitle declares.

It was also an entreaty for more writers to lighten up a bit. In my view, too many writers have an unbending attachment for veiled, somber tones (more about that later). My own rule is to try to balance heavy and light and never, ever leave anything vague.

# Sing Me!

*(A poet's call to arms)*

Sing me the words of love:
the passion, rapture and bliss
capturing hand 'n glove
Wonderland's genesis.

Sing me the fields of dreams:
the fancies, ideals and whims,
uplifting views and themes
sandcastle paradigms.

Sing me the turns of wit:
the gayness, gladness and joy,
phrases the tease and twit,
disarm, arouse, annoy.

Sing me the rush of rhyme:
the sweep and flow of verse,
music of words in time
lost art of the Universe.

## Where did all the Music go?

I lunched frequently with Mort Lewis...former manager of Simon and Garfunkle, Brothers Four and Dave Brubeck...who lived a couple of towns over. Driving to meet him one summer day, the radio news announced that Jerry Garcia of the Grateful Dead had just died.

At lunch, our waiter, a young college student on a summer job, became noticeably crestfallen when I shared the news. I was compelled to ask him what was or were the Grateful Dead's biggest hits. He couldn't recall, couldn't think of a single title.

I thought that was so indicative of so many of today's revered personalities: they are leaving no musical legacy, Footprints, yes, but as novel attractions, not musical idols. No Bennett *"San Francisco"*, Beatles *"Michele"*, Presley *"Love Me Tender"*, Streisand *"People"* Diamond *"Sweet Caroline"*, etc. Nothing.

On the drive home, the first half dozen lines of the piece that later became *"Where did all the music go?"* had been set in stone.

# Where Did All the Music Go?

Where did all the music go,
    wonderous songs we used to know?
Melodies so rich and clear,
    words of beauty, wit and cheer:
Lerner's ode to Lady Fair,
    Porter tunes so debonair,
Joyous airs of Bernstein's town
    mournful hymns of Sondheim's clowns,
Sound of Music, Carousel,
    Sgt. Pepper and "Michele"
"Love me tender", "Parsley, Sage"
    Harvests of a special age.
Out-of-date, I hear you say?
    Antiquated, so passe?

Accent now is on the beat—
    words and music of the street!
Never mind the strident verse,
    carnal dance, the rapper's curse.
Never mind the scurvy rhymes,
    it's the language of the times!
Recognize Lamar's rage,
    Idolize Beyonce's stage,
Heavy metal, Hip-Hop and punk:
    Bring on 'da noise, bring on 'da funk!

Not for me, no, not for me—
    creative mediocrity,
Yesterday held much more lure,
    artistry that will endure;
Tunes to whistle, sing, or hum,
    melody the opium.
If it's true as some expound
    all good things do come around
I hope and pray someday near
    music men will reappear,
ending then the need to know
    where did all the music go?

## Receive Me, Love...

Attending a wedding some time back, I was quite taken with the supplemental vows the bridal pair had written each other. What a neat gift, one to the other!

Why couldn't I give a similar gift to kinfolk or special friends, a verse especially written for their wedding day? And so the "Receive me, Love" idea had its origin.

Once finished, the poem is transcribed by a skilled calligrapher on antique parchment...my present to the new bride and groom.

## Receive Me, Love
*(A Wedding Canticle)*

Receive me, Love
    my essence, my oath
    encherish my pledge,
    anoint me betrothed.

Receive me, Love
    radiant I come
    undaunted my step
    unsilent my drum.

Receive me, Love
    embody me deep
    enoble my dawns
    enrapture my sleep.

Receive me, Love
    my marrow elates,
    emburnish my gift
    Elysium waits.

## It's Time to Drink the Wine...

One of my favorite work associates was a scientist from CBS Laboratories, Ben Bauer, who had the most incredible work ethic I've ever encountered, His passion was that any promising new idea or creative thought that held real potential should never linger. Otherwise, it may become fallow and, in time, worthless. Long before Nike, his credo to his associates was "Just do it!".

He was fond of wine and when he passed away shortly after retiring (an essay, yes?), I dedicated a Christmas card to his memory with a poem that connected his work spirit with his affection for wine. Held too long, wine, too, will become meritless.

I, later, submitted the poem to a national poetry competition. It garnered first prize out of several hundred entries. It contains my most favorite of all couplings..."Genesis/ Awaits its Kiss"

Usually, when a poem is finished authors find it irresistible to make changes, few poems stand where one would never change a line. For me, this is one of them.

# It's Time to Drink the Wine

Fashioned dreams
are often things
carried past their time.
Rainy days
turn yesterdays
We forget to drink the wine.


Present tense
obscures the sense
this day may be that time.
Summits hailed
stay unassailed
We forget to drink the wine.


So toast, good friend
that dream held penned
that unborn Auld Lang Syne
Genesis
awaits its kiss
It's time to drink the wine.

Our Eyes Touched in Passing...

Have you ever passed someone on the street or spied someone in a crowd and for a flashing instant your eyes met....and connected? Sure you have, we all have.

That split second harmony can sometimes be a romantic connection, sometimes intellectual or sometimes strictly congenial. Sometimes a bonding will occur, sometimes it will only be a memory, a memory where you know some connection happened, some voltage or kinship passed between you.

This is a poem that imagines an immediate amorous linkage. But it ends not in sudden bonding, rather, expectantly, in the certainty of Kismet.

And this is absolutely, positively the toughest rhyming challenge I've ever confronted. And all self-inflicted. I was stubborn about doing it in rhyme and I was wedded to the opening line and the one after. The metric beats, accents and phonetics that had to follow proved tricky and hard to manage. I also opted to insert a break in the flow i.e. 'one glance" and I became obsessed with mirroring that sound in the stanzas that followed: "by chance", romance". Whew! I could have written this in open verse in one tenth the time...but not as satisfyingly.

## Our Eyes Touched in Passing

Our eyes touched in passing
penetrating my depths,
hesitating my steps.
One glance…
indelibly lasting,
tantalizing my whole,
mesmerizing my soul,
captive of Eros' casting.

I turn, clutched in wonder,
crystallizing the view,
rhapsodizing that you
by chance…
likewise sense the thunder
disquieting your limbs
beguiling your whims,
rending all grace asunder

But no such ebb rebounds,
animating my fear-
though elatingly near-
romance…
spins merry-go-rounds.
Providently bekissed,
evidently our tryst
awaits the morrow sundowns.

Ode to Kathie Lee Gifford

In previously supervising several poetry competitions (which produced over a thousand entries) only a handful of poems aimed at the funny bone. Pity. Poetry is a wonderful medium for humor and it is puzzlingly to me why so few poets embrace it.

The bulk of poems today us of two kinds: nature paeans or solemn memory lane trips, remembrances of places, things or loved ones. Truly we don't need another poem about a beautiful autumn or sunset...as much as we need another Ogden Nash or two.

I relish fun poems. They are a joy to write and, I find, an equal joy to read or hear. Several fun poems follow, Two were prize winners (Kathie Lee and Bach to Rock) in a California competition for humor pieces.

\* \* \* \* \* \* \* \* \* \* \* \* \* \* \* \*

All of us become addicted to certain TV personalities. Their looks, their style, their believability quotient attract us. In my case, I've always had an affection for Kathie Lee with Regis Philbin. I admire her skill both as a broadcaster and as a survivor. She's bounced around a lot but has managed to keep prominent in what is undoubtedly a tough business...ergo, this vicarious, fun fantasy

\* \* \* \* \* \* \* \* \* \* \* \* \* \* \* \*

And the same endearment would go for Katie Couric or Paula Zahn.

12

# Ode to Kathie Lee Gifford

Marry me, Miss Kathie Lee,
TV goddess, fancy free!
We'll trip fantastic to the skies–
Be my music, be my rhyme,
nomad lovers lost in time,
vagabonds in paradise.

We'll waltz in Vienna,
dine in Ravenna,
savor spices of old Bombay–
ski in the Alpine snow,
kiss under mistletoe,
sip wine on the Champs Elysées!

We'll take in Octoberfest,
Black Forest and all the rest,
sail round 'n round the Greek Isles.
Our bliss will be heavenly,
paraded for all to see,
Ending only when great Buddha smiles.

Though our bond will be holy
and my pledge you'll have soley,
be advised of one little crunch:
once returned to our soil,
know you'll still have to toil…
my ardor includes no free lunch.

Choices…

My psyche loves those occasions where decisions are clear cut, open and shut. But the most rewarding judgements are those "iffy" ones that turn out to be home runs.

We've all been there…

## Choices

Black, White
　Yes, No
　　Day, Night
　　　Stop, Go

Weak, Strong
　Win, Lose
　　Short, Long
　　　Ones, Twos

Young, Old
　Rise, Fall
　　Hot, Cold
　　　Big, Small

Gay, Sad
　Dull, Bright
　　Good, Bad
　　　Left, Right

Choice is easy with extremes,
not quite so with the in-betweens.
What brings wonder to our days
is sorting out all those grays.

From Bach to Rock...

To bridge the not uncommon divide between my generation and that of my grandchildren, who, I feared, viewed me as a kind of Stone Ager. I wrote from Bach to Rock both as a lark and to prove that some of us elders can walk comfortably in other streets.

## From Bach to Rock...

Imagine if from Brahms to Bach
the classicists invaded rock...

Would Ludwig's Ninth get FM play
unless it started with "Hey, hey, hey!"

Would Mozart's best now make the grade?
None of his stuff ends in a fade.

Would Shubert's songs include a verse
to harmonize a rapper's curse?

Would Bernstein give a Blowfish hoot
if he were asked to follow suit?

Would Shubert's agent cop a plea
to finish off that symphony?

Would Copland get a big advance
for Billy Kid to do his dance?

Would "Can-Can" be called "Born to Run"
and "Water Music"...Evian?

Would Maurice Ravel become "Mo"
and Johann Strauss be known as "Yo"?

If I were a Kid Again...

Being a parent today is one of the world's toughest jobs. The liberal, non-conformist codes, the peer pressure, the affluence and more... all work against trying to mold or contain yesterday's more principled conduct.

I often wonder what kind of a kid I would be in today's indulgent, gratuitous society. I'd like to think that I wouldn't be the kind of kid described here.

Lest you think the portrait is too harsh, trust me...there's one like this in every neighborhood!

## If I Were a Kid Again

If I were a kid again, who would I be…
someone unbridled, born to be free-
free of all rules, decorum and care
life's for the good times, all else laissez-faire?

Someone with earring, unshaven, tattooed,
arrogant showboat, bearings unscrewed,
flaunting a Tee-shirt grossly X-rated,
Air Jordan Nikes, jeans perforated?

Language peppered with "wassup" and worse,
sentences mangled, littered with curse
someone with boom box bellowing rap
driving with gusto, indifferent to flap?

Tailgating demon, racing at will,
scorching of tires, my greatest thrill;
someone with lessons not ever learned
yesterday's chances pointedly spurned?

Look for no virtues beneath my veneer-
boorish, ill-mannered...no grace notes here.
The more that I ponder, the more in my gut,
the question in truth, is not "who" but what!

Rules for...

This nonsense piece came about when two of us visiting a local park, formerly a kind of swimming pond, noticed all the "no-no" signs that surrounded us: no running", "no camping", "no littering", "no drinking", "no radios" and on and on.

It conjured up for me a vision of mandated, super strict conduct at the BIG game...like the annual Yale/ Harvard classic, for decades called "The Game" Although even this would be a spoof of their meeting, some unusual disciplines can occur. Once serving as a volunteer usher, I challenged a guy who planked a cooler on a vacant seat. Unperturbed, he promptly produced a separate, extra ticket...for the cooler!

## Rules for the Well Manored Spectator at the Ultimate Game

No throwing, no crowing,
no poking, no smoking,
no moaning, no groaning
and no megaphoning.

No scowling, no growling,
no scolding, no folding,
no nodding, no prodding
and no "Oh, my Godding!"

No taunting, no flaunting,
no hamming, no damning
no staring, no glaring
and no savoir-faireing

No roasting, no boasting,
no booing, no stewing,
no bugging, no mugging
and no chugalugging,
Oh, and one more thing...

Lam Poon

This Rock 'n Roll parody was written for a poetry "slam". To those not familiar with the Slam routine, it is a performing competition wherein poets recite their work with no restriction to content before a kindred audience with selected judges grading each work until, ultimately, a winner is chosen after a group of rounds. Its conception is credited to Mark Smith, a Chicago poet, in the late 1980s who believed most poetry was too stuffy, too high-brow, too academia. His credo: "Let's make poetry interesting, understandable and fun". Once the idea caught on, it grew in popularity to where national and international competitions were held, a phenomenon that has since faded considerably in the new millennium.

I never got to perform Lam Poon in a slam but do get to share it occasionally with family and friends after a couple of Scotches.

## Lam Poon

If I painted my face and held a Fender guitar
    I could be a Rock 'n Roll star
What's so tough about this stuff
    You don't need talent, you need a schtick
It's Vaudeville that does the trick
    Kleig lights 'n skin tights
Skin heads 'n bare threads
    Bare chests 'n ripped vests    `
Leather pants and voodoo chants
    Come and get your fill
It's Vaudeville!
    And one of the most important things for fame
Is you gotta have a really, really wacko name
    TV on the Radio
Surely born out of someone's vertigo
    The Weekend
Will someone fill his fountain pen?
    5 Seconds of Summer
Getting dimmer, dumb and dumber
    And then there's Five Finget Death and The 1975
Walk The Moon 'n A Skylit Drive
    Bring Me the Horizon 'n Thunderbitch
Catfish and the Bottlemen, now isn't that rich?
    And other names so God forsaken

Real garbage…Oops, I'm sorry that, too, is taken

Truly, that is (or was) the name of a Rock 'n Roll group

Now honestly, how far can this lunacy stoop

Imagine if you're a Mom or Dad

And your kids plays in a band with a name that bad

*"And what does your son do, may I ask*

*er... He plays with Garbage"*

Is that a blast!

Oh, I know something really easy

Gotta admit it may get sleazy


I'll not only do Rock, I'll also do Rap

You know, monotone…rap a tap tap

I'll get a name that's a real zapper

I'll wear a shopping bag vest

And call myself…the Plain Brown Wrapper!

*"My brother's into crack, my sister's on the street*

*I ride my car, my Jag u ar, life is oh so sweet"*

Soon from now, you just wait and see

I'm gonna be on MTV

I won't look the same and I'll have a weird name

But from this day, I am gonna go far

Cause I'm gonna be a Rock 'n Roll Star!

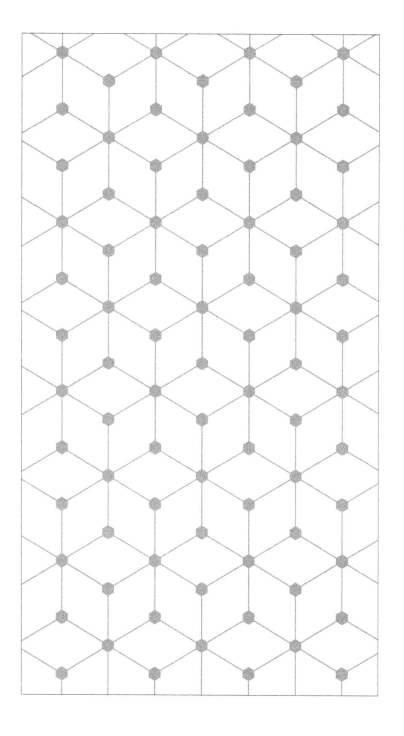

Similarities.

To me, a plane's vapor trail (contrail)...that circumstance of hot engine exhaust hitting a sudden patch of colder air...has always been a captivating sight. Seen from the ground, it is majestic, even more so from the air.

But though it starts as a thing of compelling beauty, it eventually withers and fades to obscurity.

Like lots of love affairs

## Similarities

Love
often resembles a vapor trail
It blossoms and billows-
wondrous to every eye
rapturous, entrancing,
nothing so serene.
Be it ever that way.

But no.

Imperceptibly,
adverse winds invade
edges fray
contours unweave,
bonding crumbles.
Irreparably fragmented,
it evaporates
and is
gone.

## Out of the Blue

I'm a big fan of love stories either those in print or on the screen. And I find too few genuine love stories in the poetry periodicals I track. Lots of downers sure, but few that convey the supreme joy and possible hurt of being in love.

My litmus test of a great love story is the film, Casablanca, where Humphrey Bogart and Ingrid Bergman unexpectedly meet after Bergman has left their relationship months earlier without explanation. It is one of the great love scenes ever. It is commonly known as the *"Play it again Sam"* scene. It captures the love and hurt so poignantly.

So ergo *Out of the Blue*. Casablanca it ain't but an attempt to fashion a bit of its feeling.

# Out of the Blue

I saw her again today…
We had both turned
into the same isle
at Safeway from opposite ways.
Nearly colliding,
I was ready to sputter a "sorry"
or something
only to look up
and freeze for an instant
before I could find a quick "Hi"
Seeing her
on this side of town
had been unexpected.

She said that she had worked late
and decided on some barbecued take-out
for a supper rescue.
The moment she said it
I knew,
we both knew…
she wished she hadn't.
It wasn't a time for
memories.

We had sat on a San Francisco Hill
once
looking down
on a deserted, bronze beach
tearing barbecued chicken and sourdough
with our fingers
and drinking white wine from plastic cups.
It was a golden moment then,
a sensitive remembrance now.
You could feel
her own pentium memory chip
flashing the same image.

She looked good.
She always looked good going to work
spending that extra minute or two in the morning
just to get something right
before leaving the house-
something I could never notice
but was important to her.

She had quickly followed
by asking about the cat...
how was Cleo faring,
whether she was eating well
and reminding me
about the annual shots.

Again,
she had wandered accidentally
into the settled past,
that indelible line
people like us shouldn't cross.
The timing of Cleo's annual care
always confused and eluded me
and more than once
she had jokingly admonished
that Cleo would always be living on the edge
unless she were around.

We both smiled
at the near personal broach
and began to mumble breakaways.
I know I fumbled mine.
A calm, poised
Bogart-like "See ya" exit
is the stamp
I would have liked to have left.
But...
this encounter hadn't been rehearsed.

Clumsily, I started to extend my hand
but she had anticipated the moment's awkwardness
by casually reaching for a can of coffee.
Turning to leave, she said
"Say hello to everyone"
"Sure, sure I will",
I replied, "You too."
And it was over.
She really looked good
seeing her again so
out-of-the-blue.

Lord, but I wish I hadn't.

## When the Pavement Ends

I became intrigued a bit ago with a closing sentence in a report of a season ending loss by the University of Connecticut's girls' basketball team. It read *"It's over, the pavement ends."* How cute and clever I thought. Not the journey ends or the year ends...the pavement ends. I was wondering if I could fashion something with it and stumbled on the idea of a heartbreak, a love gone South. The finality of it all. Ergo: *When the Pavement ends.*

# When the Pavement Ends

Endings never go as scripted, do they?
Dots fail to connect,
composure eludes.
Just the aching, the dying
remain absolutes.
Breaking up, surely
is the ultimate blood sport.

We dared the tides, you and I
soared with the winds of change.
Somehow a turn was missed,
fragile lanes crossed,
visions colliding,
bonding shattering,
first words forgotten,
last words ringing.

How quickly contrition rushes in—
sensing, sorting,
present and past...
Humpty Dumpty pieces
to add, multiply, divide—
eventually, inescapably,
the square root of nothingness

It's over now...
But it's not.
Your shadow
whispers, lingers;
your taste, touch
surround me still

I'm lost and adrift in yesterday.
Where do you go
when the pavement ends?

Out of Our Youth ...

I had long wanted to write a poem about WWII, a time of unparalleled valor, tragedy and yes, romance, in our history. The words "out of our youth" seemed the perfect stepping stone for what I wanted to convey: an era when America's finest surrendered their youth for their country...and never looked back.

I finished the poem coincidental with the installation of a long sought WWII memorial to be placed on Milford's green (on the 50th anniversary of Japan's surrender.)

Prior to the unveiling ceremony, I had sent the poem to our local weekly where the editor graciously printed it and where our then mayor, slated to speak at the dedication, spied it, trashed his own prepared address and opted to read the poem instead.

The mayor was pleased. The crowd seemed pleased. But no one more than I.

# Out of Our Youth
*A recognition of WWII's jubilee*

Out of our youth…we roared,
roared with a passion, muscle and sword.

Gladiators born of Depression's womb,
yesterday's children in the prime of bloom.

Striplings and sprigs now warrior men
shedding no tears for what might have been

of joys left untasted, dreams left unfilled;
time now for Country, not castles to build.

Like the youth of our fathers, innocence lost,
new tyrants to conquer, pity the cost.

Out of our youth…we stormed,
stormed the bastions and bulwarks the enemy formed:

Anzio, Iwo, Okinawa, Guam,
Normandy, Leyte, Bastogne and Luzon.

with bomber, battleships and might nonpareil,
the legions of Right met the merchants of Hell.

In more than oppression did villainy soar,
war's after-clap bared anguish that tore:

Auschwitz and Dachau, the Holocaust years,
unspeakable madness, eternity's tears.

And out of our youth…we prayed,
prayed for our dead with their dreams decayed.

Three hundred thousand gone, a million more maimed
but despots deposed, humanity reclaimed.

Conflict's cadence left no one unscarred–
heartaches, heartbreaks and mothers gold-starred.

An age badly cheated? Most will say "no".
We did what we had to, to stay freedom's glow.

If war be ordained and its purpose deemed good
This was that time when so proudly we stood.

Warbird...

A sight indelible in my mind is that of a lonely looking airship sitting silently, seemingly forsaken, on a dark, cold runway... a scene that will soon come blazingly alive as the plane launches thunderingly on its sometimes fateful purpose.

It's a scene I saw daily for months as a piloting airman in Italy (an experience I owe entirely to my brother, Vic, truly the wind beneath my wings, the catalyst who, in a wartime letter from North Africa, spurred me to try for Air Corps acceptance).

The poem was intentionally written with a transformational bent in that the scene described could easily be viewed and interpreted as that of a hawk or eagle, a true bird of prey, readying itself for the day's exploit. Reader's choice.

## Warbird

Ghostlike
in the morning mist,
it sits commandingly
on the barren tarmac,
dawn's wetness
gliding down
its powerful wings,
wings soon to lift
into the ominous overcast-
troubling, unwelcome overcast
that may obscure
the day's prey.

No matter, it will go

Lift-off readies…
Nose arching downward,
wings spanning their fullest,
it turns windward
to speed ascent.
Uncoiling bridled muscle,
its throaty roars
shatter
the daybreak's stillness
as it lifts,
lifts,
lifts,
half-circling majestically
a flawless chandelle,
disappearing
into the embracing shroud,
never to return.

Pity

Mediterranean Remembrance

Mid-way during an airman's combat tour, it is usually a time for what the military terms 'R'n R'', rest and relaxation. Airmen in Italy were favored with a hiatus in what many believe may be one of the most beautiful places in the world, Capri, a tiny mountainous Isle a few miles from Naples.

This trip down memory lane recalls one evening when a group of airmen enjoying the comforts of the Hotel Quissana ventured to the nearby town square, La Piazzetta, for wine and merriment which suddenly turned somber.

# Mediterranean Remembrance
*(Once upon a time in Capri, December 44)*

Maybe it was the surrounding lamp lights
suddenly illuminating the dim, garlanded square,
piercing the melancholy aura,
bonding mood and moment-

or simply an airman's nostalgic quickening...

his wavering, tenor voice,
hesitant, hardly audible,
drifting across the enlivening plaza
  *"Si – lent night, ho – ly night"*

slowly joined in ragged unison
by mingling revelers,
  *"All is calm"*

subordinates and superiors,
majors and minors.
all, now, comrades in common-
  *"All is bright"*

here, lifting Chiantis in noble tribute
there, waving glowing cigarettes
baton fireflies-
to the gentle melody and meter.
  *"Round yon vir – gin"*

For some it would be their last night
on the ancient, elevated square,
  *"Mo – ther and child"*

the end of their mid-mission tour
before their return to Squadrons X, Y and Z.
  *"Ho – ly in – fant"*

'R and R', rest and relaxation,
the military manuals called it,
   *"So ten – der and mild"*

the required intermission
to relieve mission fatigue,
   *"Sleep in Hea – ven – ly peace"*

Savored moments of detachment
treasured to the extreme.
   *"Sle - ep in Hea - ven - ly peace"*

No sooner finished,
the angelic hymn, less haltingly
began again.

This time,
voices more unified,
some solemn. others assertive,
echoes of differing yesterdays.

How ironic,
a song of adversative birth*...
no matter, it was now a universal gift–
every warrior's anthem
of home and serenity.

Cherished. Hallowed.

*Stille Nacht, 1818. Original German lyrics, Rev. Josef Mohr; melody, Franz Gruber.

Beyond Words…

A few years ago, I fulfilled a long held ambition of walking the streets of the German and Austrian cities I had once bombed: Munich, Salzburg, Innsbruck and more. To look down from Innsbruck's Olympian ski jump at the downtown rail yards I had bombed twice was truly a moving experience.

Part of the excursion included visits to the death camps of Dachau and Buchenwald…each, now, a public museum. More sobering moments. Nothing has been sanitized, the full horrors of the Holocaust are not spared.

I was particularly disturbed by Buchenwald. It is nestled deep in a picture-book forest adjacent the gentle town of

Weimar, for centuries Germany's cultural center where many of history's greatest artists lived and gathered. The juxtaposition was pointedly troubling…two extremes, side by side.

I knew I wanted to write about Buchenwald but wasn't sure quite how till a friend, Jack Merrell (his wife, Rosemary, is aka Rosemary Rice, stage and TV actress, notably the *"I Remember Mama"* series and recording artist of children's fare) encouraged me to focus on the contradictory aspect. After several attempts, I chose to introduce the very strange Weimar/Buchenwald incongruity like an off-stage commentary. Do read it that way to capture the irreconcilability and illogicalness that bothers me still.

## Beyond Words

Step by step
the great, unfolding cinder fields
render
a piercing crunch underfoot,
conjuring visions
of marshalled strides-
heavy, sinister, purposeful.

Gone
the demonic barracks,
once teeming with withered souls,
reduced now to ash
But one remains.
a chilling sentry to the past.

> *And the nearby, good people of Weimar,*
> *home of their beloved Goethe,*
> *rendezvous court of Brahms, Chopin, Schumann-*
> *what crunch did they hear?*

The ghostly, placid assembly yard
rouses gripping echoes
of ominous morning roll-calls
daily lottery of finality.

The Krematorium
stands as before:
unhidden, undisguised,
six massive ovens
adjacent inhuman, entr'acte passage-
stark, black hooks
speared
into bleak, concrete walls,
walls forever entombed
with the sound of deliverance.

> *Pity the lost voices of Weimar,*
> *entrapped in their anguish of survival;*
> *your Presidential streets proffer visible lament,*
> *enduring penance for yesterday 's silence.*

Buchenwald…
All, now, a museum,
museum whose only admission
is that one sees
and remembers
a time…
    beyond madness,
        beyond depravity,
            beyond words.

*(Countless streets and avenues in Weimar have been*
*renamed for American presidents: Washington, Lincoln,*
*Kennedy, etc.)*

I was Young Once…

Watching the Olympics on TV some years ago, I had a vision of someone elderly, captivated by the youthful energy, purpose and triumph of the contestants, pausing to wonder if he, or she, had made the most of their own youth. The vision quickly accelerated to a concept that began to write itself.

Shortly afterward, my oldest, closest friend, Ed Carroll, died suddenly. We had met in our twenties as fellow record salesmen, he RCA, I Columbia, immediately bonding a tight relationship the continued to the day he died.

Asked by his family to speak at his funeral, I chose to read the newly written poem for its serendipitous fit, proper praise for a man who, from modest beginnings, succeeded tellingly all his life, personally and professionally.

This somber experience was also a harbinger, in part, for the later poem, *Nightfire*.

Having openly shared this, it has taken on a life of its own as a frequently employed eulogy by others.

## I Was Young Once

I was young once…
Did I make the most of it,
try to make the pieces fit?
Did I learn to try enough,
set my goals up high enough?
Did I stand tall to reach the crown
or rise again when I was down?
Was I there when crisis called
and did I give my utmost all?
I was young once
Did I have that great romance-
storybook, charmed happenstance?
Did I teach my children right
steer clear the dark, embrace the light?
Was I a cause of kindness spurned-
a deed, a favor unreturned?
Did I thank God for gifts acquired:
good health, true love and friendships sired?

\* \* \* \* \* \*

As seasons fade, we dare to size
the plus and minus of our lives,
to gauge the good and what was not,
the feats and failures of our lot.
I'd like to think as days burn late
and second chances hesitate.
with heart and soul, mind and tongue,

I did my best when I was young.

Nightfire...

All of us have had those tormenting times over a wringing sick watch or the passing of a loved one or the painful ending of a friendship or love affair, the heartbreak of losing a treasured pet...and such. You torture yourself with imagining that if you or someone could have done or said this or that then everything could be put back together again, like Humpty Dumpty.

Nights are endless. The respite of sleep never comes. The throbbing never stops. It is a thoroughly piercing experience.

Morning comes with no comfort in sight. Just more of the same and, most likely, worse.

# Nightfire

I wake
to echoes of the night before-
Or did I sleep at all?
My temples hammer and throb,
the wadded pillow,
perversely,
amplifies the pounding
a sounding board
incessantly thundering.

I could not have slept;
I remember no dream.
Only...
voices, gestures, expressions,
swirling and fusing,
dissolving
swirling and fusing again,
a racking endless loop,
unerasable recollections
mercifully wished to be erased-
expunged, removed...forgotten.
Would that my inner being
regain its peace
untroubled, unmarked
like the page unwritten upon.
Yet the tormenting images persist,
indelible, they burn and blister
withering my psyche, my soul.

Daylight penetrates,
my despair intensifies;
the full morning
painfully is here.

## Breakfast with Bach

The New York Times in one of its opinion pages once ran a pencil outline of Manhattan with an essay about the Island written within the boundries. At that time I was pondering the theme of my annual Christmas/Holiday card enclosure and thought I would do something similar. I chose my Sunday morning wake-up routine written within the form of a musical note. It became a pretty good hit.

# Breakfast with Bach

Sleepily, I punch on the CD
Hey, did Bach know how to
write wake up music or what?
Trumpets
do the trick
Baroque
Clarions-
just like
coffee,
speaking
of which
it's gotta be
ready by
now. Won-
der if the
paper's here
and how
the Uconn
girls did
Wonderful!
And would
ya believe
the fore-
cast? Hey
they owe us.
Man, is this
good Danish or what? Bach
and Breakfast. Wonder how he
got his juices started: pheasant eggs
over light with steaming tea? And did
he care about sports? Did Salzburg
beat Vienna in lawn bowling? They
did it? Damn, there goes six ducats,
Here's to you, Johann. You're the
best Where's my cup? Is this a
great Sunday morning
or what?

With acknowledgment to R. Peter Munves for borrowing the title of his best selling CD

What would Sister Gertrude Say?...

Not long ago in my little tranquil town, High school kids stormed out of their mid-day classes and marched to Town Hall in protest of some new rules affecting their wearing of baseball caps during school hours. Certain logo hats were not allowed, others ok.

I went nuts. Baseball caps in class! And a protest over some logo curbing! I climbed all over my Board of Ed reps. I couldn't help but think of my own school days where we, as a matter of course, toed the line, especially in those few years I had attended parochial school. You never, ever, wanted to get out of line with Sister (Mary) Gertrude. You were convinced that Hell couldn't be worse than her wrath and ruler.

I know, I know...that was then, this is now. Times change, things change. But I've often wondered how Sister Gertrude would react to today's environment. I intended to make her reaction a fun piece but I'm having writer's block...all I've done, so far, is paint the picture she'd be facing, a picture I thought worthwhile sharing. For now look upon this as a kind of work-in-progress.

(Incidentally, all baseball caps are now banned in school as are jackets with gang type logos). Happy day.

## What would Sister Gertrude say?

What would Sister Gertrude think
of shaven heads and pants that sink
beneath the norms of dignity?
Of facial rings and lewd tattoos
stenciled shirts, Air Jordan shoes
and other scorns of prudery?
Of beepers, pagers, laser-lights
iPhones, iPads, classroom fights
and unrepentant truancy?

What would Sister Gertrude say
of social graces in decay,
demeanor void of decency?
Of failing grades that trouble few
and condom doles that ballyhoo
student taunts of sovereignty?
Of pregnancies and disrespect,
abdicated intellect
and self-destruction destiny?

Song for Avery

I got so enamored of an absolutely adorable photo of a new great
grandchild that it commanded me to share it, with some suitable prose,
with family and friends as a Christmas card enclosure. Ergo, Song
for Avery. Similarily, on the receiving end, mine was always a most
welcoming mailbox drop for annual holiday photos.

## Song for Avery

*May sunbeams grace your every morn, moonbeams still your night, gleams from heaven hold you warm, angels tend your fright. May rosebuds be your coverlet, orchid blooms your down as fairies dance and pirouette and leprechauns surround. Tinker Bell will be there too, with 'pixie' dust in hand; together on a kangaroo, you'll fly to Neverland. Slumber, slumber, Little One and wake to golden glim. Morning's music has begun and waits your joining in.*

The Game of Names

When my newly married youngest granddaughter and her husband were expecting their family addition, they pledged not to know their baby's gender until the first wail. In the interim, the family had great fun anticipating and guessing the arrival and suggesting names

My own vibe was certain that the child would be a girl and I, accordingly, immersed myself in slugging away at finding a suitable one or two syllable name, the parent's preference, to go with the family name. It was then that I got quite taken with the fashion evolution of girl's names over the years, converting my research into a humorously informing Christmas card enclosure. But the research proved moot...

Came the eventual day, the parents welcomed Liam.

# The Game of Names
*(Times change, things change…so do names)*

Some decades ago when Roll Call came
It was always Mary, Helen, Dorothy, Jane
Margaret, Frances, Shirley and Ruth
Favorite monikers of yesteryear's youth
Fashions that stayed for a very long spell
Till Hollywood' s dawn brought new personnel
Katherine, Elizabeth, and lots of Junes
leading the rush for new nom de plumes
Linda, Nancy and Susan by-the-swarm
Like daughter Susan having twelve more in her dorm
And Barbara, Lisa, Jessica and Kate
A whole host of new names to assimilate
But slowly, slowly, they, too lost their glow
To the new torrent of boomers hot on-the-go
Enter Jennifer, Kelly, Madison, Michelle
Stephanie, Kimberly, Amy, Isabelle
Later came Morgan, Meghan, Ashley and Mia
Brittany, Emma, Emily, Sophia
Then millennium comes with the query "What's new?"
Well, my kinfolk Brynn's graduation list offers a clue
It pointedly shows how far we have come
with no names from the past, not even one
No Mary, no Helen, no Frances, no Jane
But a whale of new candidates vying for fame
Two in particular catch anyone's glance
The first is Sierra, looming forerunner by chance?
The other for vogue is hardly germane
The name is November, with middle name Rain.

The Diamond...

Story poems are another wasteland. Another pity. The beat and
rhythmic flow of poetry make for a perfect way to tell a story. It is sad
that virtually the only use of story rhyme today is with the rap idiom.

Diamond had a strange origin. The catalyst was the click/clack sound
of the daily train taking me home. Commuters are normally inured
to the rumble of rail tracks, never really conscious of the sound. But
if you allow yourself to think about the click-clacking...really embrace
it...you begin to sense a kind of musical dit/dot, dit/dot beat, not
unlike the under rhythm of a lot of Johnny Cash things.

One such time, the dit/dot, sing/song pattern got into my head and I
began to conjoin it with random, rhyming words, the words began to
take on form....and the essence for the Diamond came to be.

The experience of rhythm becoming the occasion of something of
structure and substance is not that unusual, I found. I, later, narrated a
bio of Cole Porter for a state program of Readings for the Blind (one
of 38 books I've read and recorded as a volunteer) where I learned that
many of his songs simply started with the rhythm. Before any words or
music, he would first establish a beat of intrigue...and the rest followed

Diamond plays best if you imagine an Irish or Scottish accent as you
read it. (I've learned that in the occasional public readings I've done).
My rainy day ambition (of many!) is to keep extending the story line, a
saga of more twists and turns.

# The Diamond

A diamond is a precious thing, a treasure of the heart,
a symbol of undying love and dreams that never part...

This story tells of Michael Wells, a Scottish lad from Kone
who traveled down Pretoria town to find his dreams in stone
The diamond filled a hundred mil, the biggest ever known,
he packed his grip and hailed a ship and quick he took it home.

His love did cry when by-and-by her eye did spy the cast.
"Its yours", he said, "me lovely Red. 'till death it seals us fast".
No surer word was ever heard when in her hands it twitched:
the diamond shone and burned her bone and she lay still bewitched.

And later on, another dawn, he met Miss Molly Cloth.
His eyes did shine, "I'll make her mine, this stone will seal our troth"
And seal it did her pretty lid when it shone upon her face
that very day she fell away, no breath was there a trace.

He cried and vexed, "The diamond's hexed, no love it's meant to know.
Oh Lord within, it's filled with sin, it casts a Devil's glow!"
He made a vow no more would bow beneath that evil stone:
he sealed it up and spilled the cup of dreams he might have known.

A diamond is a precious thing, a treasure of the heart,
a symbol; of undying love and dreams that never part.

## Manhattan Morning

I can honestly say that it was exceedingly rare for me to ever have a
Blue Monday. For two reasons. I truly loved doing what I did in the
recording field .and where I did it...in the most exciting and complete
city in the world, New York. I've been priviledged to have spent time
in many of the great cities of the world and none has the robust
vibrancy and universality of New York. None. London may have
its crisp stateleness, Paris its fanciful charm, Rome its time-honored
granduer. But New York is supreme. Any wonder it's suitably called
The Big Apple.

## Manhattan Morning

Stepping
into midtown's
vibrant, muscular air,
the electricity is enwrapping
animated, restless, surging streets
pulsating
with tempo and tension,
handmaids of commerce dawning.

Dodging
militant taxis
morning pushcarts
night people homeward bound,
the day's Warriors-
clerks, secretaries, executives,
clutching buttered rolls and coffee
stride hurriedly,
glancing at bargain windows,
racing bustling crossings
musing of the night before,
preoccupied with the day ahead.

Behind
corporate gateways,
shuttered store fronts,
silent marquees,
diverse agendas begin igniting-
mega mergers, company couips,
First editions, fashion revolts.
ultimate auctions, sidewalk sales
stage rehearsals, agency reviews,
grand openings, legal settlements.
All in place..
The business
of Manhattan's business
has reached lift-off.

Damn You Roget!

That elusive word…anyone doing writing or public speaking has faced that dilemma, it is especially tormenting composing traditional poetry.

Sometimes it never comes despite *Roget's Thesaurus* or *Rodale's Synonym* search and that may become a cause to scrub an important thought and strike for a new viewpoint or concept. Or try fudging something however zany like Larry Hart, early lyrist for Richard Rodgers, did to rhyme Philadelphia with "go to hell for ya".*

*Acknowledgment: A Ship without a Sail, Gary Marmorstein, Simon and Schuster.

# Damn You Roget!

Where or where lies that peerless word
That missing gem that eludes
that butterfly on tip of tongue
  that connects, connotes, concludes?

Damn you Roget, just spit it out
that word away from bliss
Speak, affirm, assert, announce
Perfection's Genesis.

Regrettably, the search goes on
still void of final close
 a shifty, slipp'ry leprechaun
deaf to the call of Prose.

Tomorrow stirs, it's getting late
this maddening circumstance
Numbs the mind and energy
Done in by wordplay dance.

Surely, the morn will vent the prey
veiled like dust in cloth
enabling that elusive word
to make the Whole betrothed.

## Perplexity

Some years ago when I moved into my newly constructed home, a beautiful Colonial on a one acre lot, a friend came by with a soda box (remember them?) of just plucked pachysandra. It was a most appropriate gift since we hadn't started any landscaping and we needed something to cover the bare ground where an inground oil tank had just been installed in the side yard. The pachysandra covered the spot beautifully. Other than an initial watering, the patch was left to care for itself. And did it ever! In its first year, the patch had grown and spread by more than half with no care...no watering, no fertilizing, nothing. Within a few more years, the patch had turned the corner and spread along the back of the house and yard, Whoa! I realized then I had better start grooming and began edging the spread with my mower. No dice. It was impervious to cutting. The same with weed killer, the same with an extended drought. It just keeps growing and going as it pleases.

The only remedy to stop a pachysandra spread is to hand pluck each plant cleanly, leaving no trace of a root. You have been forewarned.

# Perplexity

Princeton said "'No', as did Harvard and Yale
Entreaties to all were of little avail
likewise Stanford, Cornell and MIT
We've been there before without remedy"

"The problem, Sir, is it's idiopathic"
All mourned in turn, quite melodramatic.
No known cause, no known cure,
Grin and bear it, learn to endure

I won't buy defeat, I pledged to myself
There must be a way to get needed help.
Ah, the Internet!, That's the solution.
Answers galore with full attribution.

But even the cyber Gods proved non affecting
A puzzle they said beyond their dissecting.
But there must be some way, must surely be
No sticky wicket is gonna stop me.

What about asking IBM's Watson?
Master of clues, it surely must got some
No problem yet has stymied this learner

Word quickly returned, it's on the back burner
Till then, I'll just keep saying my mantra
Cause soon we'll all know how to halt…

(Now all together) **Pachysandra!**

Snowstorm on Country Lane

Is there anything more intoxicatingly beautiful than a day's dawning after a night's snowfall. I've been blessed to have lived on a country lane of breathtakingly winter beauty after a snowfall, a happening that always fostered a quick dash for the camera to capture indelibly the matchless, luminous scene. I never, ever tired of it.

## Snowstorm on Country Lane

Softly, silently
The first flakes fall
Glistening the grass,
Feather-dusting the road.
Gently
The bordering brush whitens-
Soon,
Ground pine and periwinkle vanish.
Across the way
In the thickening light,
A frolicsome Schnauzer,
Truant since midday,
Celebrates drunkenly,
The quickly deepening snow

Night brings winter's rogue: wind
Muscular, menacing.
Bellowing with thunderous rush,
It rips downward
Churning,
Foaming
Spewing,
Whipping all in its way-
Crashing at road's end
Against defiant hemlocks.
Limbs grind and bend,
Some too much,
Splintering in vanquished agony.

Trailing the wind's drive
The billowing wake
Spins curliques
Around every standing thing.
With each sweep
Drifting rims the roadsides
Bushes mounds into globes.
Nightlong...
The wind streaks
Stabbing, twisting-
Sculpting its whim,
Carving its way
Till its exhaustive
Aftermost gust...

Dawn illuminates winter's nativity,
Natures' ultimate expression
Nothing earthly so wondrous,
Nothing.
Every tree and branch
An ivory silhouette;
Lawns, unblemished snow fields;
Rooftops, mushroomed snow cones;
Swanlike curvatures here,
Angular Picasso patterns there.
Everything, everywhere
Virgin white
Flawless, Immaculate, Majestic.

Tingle, Tangle

This is a story framed from a bit of reality, as are two others that follow. For a lot of years. thirty in all to be exact, I commuted from my home in Connecticut to Manhattan daily, normally a 90 minute ride, sometimes longer. On one occasion, my foot fell asleep, numb as a brick, just before disembarking and I had a devil of a time getting out of my seat and hobbling my way thru Grand Central Station. It taught me to tamp my feet now and then on subsequent runs so as to avoid similar bummers. And ergo, an idea came for a story.

# Tingle, Tangle

"Playing footsie again? Shame," the intruder said jokingly.

The man was clearly embarrassed. Caught rubbing toes behind a desk, who wouldn't be? But he had to. The damn toes were tingling again. Not sore, not aching–just tingling. He first had walked around his desk trying to shake it off as he would a foot fallen asleep. Next, he gently stomped his foot in the carpet. No help. That's when, in frustration, he took off his shoe and–enter his associate.

He told his wife about the incident when he came home. She found it amusing and dismissed it as quickly as her flashing smile. But he didn't. Throughout dinner, he said little. He was trying to remember when the tingling first started. It had been going on for a few days but could it have been longer? He remembered developing a sense of it casually. Just a little ripple of a sensation, not unpleasant, a kind of an untroubling prickle in his left toes, all of them. Then the sensation had gone. But had it — or had it gone simply because he didn't think about it? Like a care that disappeared when it's not thought of, or a freckle that isn't a bother until it's seen. The tingling, he speculated, could have been going on for more than a few days, before he had given it any thought. The problem now was that he thought about it alot. However, he was from a school that maintained unless it hurts or bleeds, it will go away, so having it looked at was out of the question. The tingling, he reassured himself, didn't really trouble him physically. It annoyed him. That's what really bothered him, that it was consuming much of his attention. The tingling never left him or his consciousness. Whatever he was doing, his mind would invariably break ranks and take a reading. Yes, it was there it was always there.

He started employing little responses whenever the tingling pierced his awareness. On the train ride to work he would occasionally stomp his heel downward on the floor as if he were trying to dislodge an imaginary clump of clay from his shoe. He would do the same thing walking, striking his heel just a little harder for a few steps every so often. Working behind his desk or sitting at a meeting, he began the habit of tapping a pencil against his shoe. That often provoked an unsettling parallel thought: Did he really feel the pencil tap? Or had the tingling numbed his toes? He would tap harder to make sure which. Convinced that he felt them both, he would abandon the practice only to resume it later for a new confirmation.

He began to mention the sensation—offhandedly, like small talk or a throw-away comment. When his associates at lunch popped a couple of vitamin pills, he opined that maybe that's what he also should do to remedy his "sleepy" foot —jazz up his circulation. No emphasis or added comment was made to generate an inquiry and his remark vaporized in the sweep of luncheon talk. But somehow he felt better by giving it notice. Small as it was, he began to do the same thing with other associates at other times. Just a casual reference which varied with his mood. A "crazy tingle" it was called sometimes, at others wisecracking that his leg "felt like a damn clubfoot." Always smilingly, always laid back. Nothing to turn the flow of conversation, nothing to prod a rejoinder although he was hoping for one. He wished someone would say that, yes, he had that once and it drove him bugs for a couple of days. But no one did. All he got was a transient smile and the matter faded.

At home, it became a light-hearted topic, his wife asking him how his "little tingle" was upon greeting. When the kidding had run its course, she one day suggested that maybe he should have it checked since it had been hanging on. He felt sheepish at the thought. He still had no reason to think it was serious. He just assumed that like an itch or rash he would wake up one day and it would be gone. So no need for a doctor. But he compromised by saying he would call. And he did.

The doctor's first response to the recital about the foot was that he should come in about the ailment, downplayed now to a "tickle" but when the man repeatedly made light of his call, finally apologizing for its bother, the doctor, with enduring resignation, ended the conversation by cautioning him to come in if the matter changed.

But it didn't.

Nor did his acquired mannerisms: the heel striking, the pencil tapping, the occasional reference. It was a lifestyle ingrained into his being. And the routine tranquilized him. While he still gave the tingling as much attention as before, the anxiety over giving it attention lessened. His routine of responding to the tingling became steady, automatic. He now did it all unthinkingly and therefore without notice to himself. But not to his associates. They noted how his gait changed, how his manner at meetings became less composed with his rhythmic pencil tapping of his stubbing against the table leg. Out of earshot, some of the junior executives began referring to him as "Mr. Tingle Toe".

His wife noticed the peculiarities too. Her sympathetic, indulgent manner gave way to detachment and finally to irritation. "Why don't you have it checked again?" She asked pointedly.

Soberingly, in a flash, he had to agree, it didn't bother him but it bothered her. And maybe, just maybe, it could be bothering him and he didn't know it. Like an early warning sign to a back problem, or a circulatory ailment which he had joked about just to make conversation. He would do it—he would have it looked at, assuring her he would do it the next day. Besides, he admitted to himself, he hadn't slept well since the tingling started.

"The blood's ok, so are the neurological responses. So are the x-rays. It may be just a seasonal abberation of no consequence," the doctor reported by phone the day after the exam "needing no more than sunshine and exercise. Feet relish fresh air like anything else. Ever walk around bare footed?" He said he did but more than that he related that one of his simple joys was puttering around his lawn barefoot even, on occasion, playing Frisbie with his neighbor sans shoes. The doctor encouraged him to keep it up, said he would phone a prescription for a sedative to the man's pharmacist and wished him a "Happy New Year," some five months away.

Relieved of his concern and peace made at home, he started concentrating on not responding to the tingle—which still persisted, enhanced exercise, fresh air and all, Each time he caught himself about to make an old response, he would focus totally on not making one, It became a game he played at work or on the train—to see how long he could hold out before giving in to the exquisite pleasure of stomping his foot or stubbing his toe. Just a few taps immediately followed by another try. He would set a marker on the train of so many minutes or so many stops and when he succeeded his frequent, silent grins sometimes would catch a puzzling look from fellow commuters. He found that he could think so hard that he often would not later remember reading parts of the morning paper though he knew he had gone methodically through every page.

Walking to work, his mind pointedly fixed on a steady, even gait, he twice nearly walked against a light into an oncoming bus.

His associates couldn't help but immediately notice the change. Whereas his manner before was one of constant fidgeting and motion, he now seemed remote. Mesmerized. At meetings, he would require a jog, sometimes several, before he responded with attention to something directed to him. He found that he could fix his mind so totally on the tingling and non-response, controlling his feet and hands from any former motion whatever, as to perceive he had no limbs at all. Only a mind. A mind capable of inducing non-feeling. A mind powerful and so finely tuned as to leave his body at will. His frequent stoic, half-conscious appearance became a topic of office gossip, leading some of his associates to wonder if he were taking something more than a martini at lunch.

It wasn't long after that his wife received a call unbeknownst to him, from an office friend asking if everything was, well, sort of all right. The incident chilled her. Previously, she had supposed that the reassuring physical examination would have soon ended the aberrant mannerisms. But she knew it had not. Instead one eccentricity had been replaced by another. and, now, it was fully public. And threatening. She hastily submitted to the friend that her husband's temporary program of exercise and medication doubtlessly made him act listless at times but that, yes, everything is or would be "all right." But privately she feared that it wasn't physical at all, rather that some psychological irregularity had invaded his lifestyle; something the doctor didn't detect the first time but would the second.

Getting him to go again was less a problem than she expected. The logic of a follow-up visit was not contested. That a strain had come into their relationship the man knew but he felt that it was she who had tuned him out, she who had caused a breach with her less than understanding attitude. Whereas otherwise he would have argued her suggestion about a second visit, to show her that he was cooperative and tolerant, he agreed that another visit was maybe a good idea.

"What do you mean, an interview?" he testily asked the doctor in response to the suggestion that the man visit a colleague. "Just 'cause my toes tingle, I should see a shrink? You mean I'm imagining all this?"

"Heavens, no." the doctor replied. "Only that the nervous system is a very special field and it's worth checking out when there is no muscular or skeletal abnormalty. Nerves play funny tricks on the body. Neuropsychiatry isn't what you may think it is."

He bridled at the thought that the tingling was illusory. The toes did tingle. He knew that—why in hell didn't they know that. He was doubly angered at the challenge to his credibility and at being entrapped in his commitment to see the matter through. Medicine's running amuck, he thought.

No simple answers anymore, no simple cures. A guy comes in with a toe problem and they say it's his head. They have the body pieced into so many parts that pretty soon they'll have doctors simply to tell you what doctor to go to. One visit, that's all, he averred. One visit to this foot or head doctor and that's it. It's easier to live with the problem than the runaround.

The arranged visit didn't go well. He had become so mistrustful of other's reactions to what he allowed was a patently simple discomfort that he was hostile and guarded in discussing it.

Despite the doctor's calm prodding, he remained terse and ill-tempered, "Let the son-of-a-bitch tell me what it is, not the other way around," he fumed silently.

But the doctor only had questions—questions which merely irritated him more. At the end of a mutually taxing hour, the doctor declared that he would organize some "tests" for the next visit. Leaving as belligerent as he had come, the man feigned interest, knowing he would not return. As the man left, the doctor scribbled in his diary: "uncommunicative—deep-rooted anticivility phobia—psychological testing needed to validate therapy direction." Not a word about tingling toes.

For the man, nothing changed. Not at home, nor at the office. Anger abounded within him. Anger at his wife for remaining detached. Anger at his associates at his discovery of their clandestine mockery. Anger at the doctors for their unenlightenment. But most of all, anger at himself for his inability to devise a coping routine: whether to respond to the tingle or ignore it—and how. The thought of reacting to it brought instantly the derision of "Mr. Tingle Toe" to mind while the problem with ignoring it meant that the only way to leave it alone was to think about leaving it alone—tuning out — and that he knew was an equally troubling alternative. At every turn, it was no win.

But he did find some small comfort. It came in the security of being alone. He began shunning fellow commuters. He quit all business luncheons. He avoided neighborhood mingling. He hardly spoke at home, from day to night, his objective was to be by himself as much as possible. His wife saw that their ever-widening estrangement was no longer by her initiative but his. She sensed the worst. Reading every change in his conduct as deterioration to an inevitable break-down, she counseled with both doctors, arriving with their affirmation to what seemed the inescapable conclusion: professional rest and therapy.

He made no protest at the suggestion. He welcomed it. He relished the thought of escaping home and work and the opportunity for greater solitude. His consenting behavior so disarmed his wife that she was sure another downturn was imminent. The need for professional help, she believed, had been organized in the nick of time.

At the retreat, he was paired with a roommate—part of his therapy to encourage opening up—whom he found likeable and not intruding, his need for convalescence brought on by despondency and overwork in trying to save, unsuccessfully, a family business from collapse.

The days were occupied and tranquil: group lectures on loving and relationships, reading from the limited library selection, once a group rap session at which he didn't speak but which he found quietly exhilarating, an evening movie, usually a musical or a comedy, and lots of liberty time to stroll around the soundless grounds. After the third day it occurred to him that he was thinking less about the tingling and the events that brought him there and more about the next day's routine. Occasionally, for the swiftest second, a thought flickered that the tingling had momentarily stopped—but he dismissed it as imaginary. By week's end he was sleeping without a sedative, something he hadn't done for six weeks.

It was during one of those sleeps when the dawn fire began. No one detected its start. By the time an aide leisurely enjoying morning coffee in the quiet lounge noticed the smoke, the maintenance wing to the rear of the building was glowing and crackling with spreading flames. The aide reacted quickly. With his shouting and sounding of the alarm, the building came alive with other half-dressed aides and administrators running to their emergency posts, and heads poking down hallways searching for confirmation that there was indeed a fire and the need to vacate was real.

The man and his roommate, hearing the alert and attendant commotion, and sensing instantly the realities of events, moved as one to exit their room to the prescribed fire drill position on the entrance lawn. Grabbing jackets and a few personals, they ran barefooted out of the building to the spacious front lawn wet with the morning's dew. As they jogged, pajama-clad, across the sodden turf, looking back at times to see the billowing flames, his roommate's face grew pained with each step. In a flash the man thought "Coronary!"—slowing to make ready to assist. But to his surprise, the roommate plodded on quickly blurting to him in a grieving, sideways glance, "Geez, wet grass: Now my toes will be tingling for weeks!"

Heart to Heart

This actually happened to a friend of mine and Voila—another premise for a story. He had copied the Power Ball numbers out of the paper believing he had connected on four of the five numbers (plus Power Ball) only to discover he had but three not four. Some difference!

# Heart by Heart

"Wake up, Babe, wake up!"

*"Um...er...wha...what?"*

"Wake up, big news"

*"What's happened? Something's Happened!"*

"Something important!"

*"You're scaring me."*

"We're rich!"

*"RICH?"*

"Yes, rich. We won the lottery"

*"The lottery?"*

"That's what I said...the lottery"

*"Powerball?"*

"Not quite. Kind of second place"

*"No joking?"*

"No joking"

*"Whoa!"*

"Yep. lots of money"

*"What's a lot?"*

"Hundreds of thousands...
Maybe a million. Maybe more"

*"You sure?"*

"Cross my heart"

*"How do you know for sure?"*

"Saw my numbers on the early news
just now. Got all five right except
for Powerball"

*"And you're sure?"*

"Hope to die"

*"We gotta tell the kids."*

"No, no, let's wait"

*"Wait? Wait for what?"*

"The lotto Website. It'll be up
soon. It'll tell us how much"

*"And you said a lot"*

"New cars for us, the kids and
their kids. And a whole,
whole lot more"

*"Like staying at that Tuscan
villa again"*

Or right next to George
Clooney's if you want"

*"I still can 't believe it"*

And we'd join the club. No
more condo and public courses'"

*"Count me in"*

"Some Christmas, huh? "

*"Best ever"*

"Perfect timing"

*"We could spend Christmas in
Florence. Always dreamed of that"*

"Or New Year's in Paris"

*"And fly first class?"*

"Anything for you, Babe"

*"Dear, are you really, really sure"*

"Really sure. Know my numbers
by heart Seven, fourteen, nineteen,
twenty seven, thirty"

*"All our birthdays...how lucky"*

"We'll know any minute now"

*"I still cannot believe it"*

"Here. here it comes"

*"My coffee is shaking"*

"Damn!"

*"What...what ?"*

"Damn! Damn! Damm!" "

*"What's wrong...something's wrong!"*

"It's ONE..., fourteen, nineteen,
twenty-seven, thirty. Not seven!
I must have read it too fast and
kinda went blank!"

*"What does that mean?"*

"Everything!"

*"With just one number different?"*

"Yes, like Prince to Pauper"

*"But there 's still a prize, yes?"*

"Yes, but I hate to tell you"

*"But it still must be pretty nice"*

"Two hundred dollars"

*"You really are joking this time.*
*Tell me you're joking"*

"No, it's just two hundred dollars"

*"And what would we have won?"*

"Two million"

*"Two million!"*

"That's what it says"

*"That doesn't seem fair"*

"I know…some zany law of math…"

*"Still doesn't seem fair"*

"From Prince to Pauper"

*"Lucky we never called the kids"*

"Seems nutty to say. But in a way,
that's a real Christmas present"

*"Funny how we count blessings".*

"That truly would have been
a train wreck"

*"There goes our Italy, Paris, the*
*country club and my Audi"*

"I'm so sorry I screwed up."

*"Number I can sometimes look like 7.*
*But you sure did give us quite a ride"*

"We really were on kind of
a high, weren't we."

*"Like I was five again believing in*
*Santa Claus"*

"I'll be tough getting over this".

*"Santa is forever when you 're five.
This, I'll get over. Truth be told, it
never really had a chance to sink in"*

"So. you're ok"

*"I'm ok.*

"No fibbing?"

*"No fibbing"*

"What say we go somewhere.
Anywhere… And first class."

*"Deal!"*

"Merry Christmas, Babe"

*"Merry Christmas, Sluggo"*

First in Line

Another story patterned from a true experience. I spotted an ad once in my morning paper about a big sale in an electronics store scheduled for Thanksgiving weekend. A really big sale cautioned with 'Limited supplies'. I needed a new tuner for my hi-fi rig and made a plan to be among the first in line come Friday when the store opened. I got there early as intended. What a surprise!

# First in Line

"You're up early"

Looking up from his morning paper, the man was clearly surprised. His wife's morning routine was always later than his own but here she was sauntering into the kitchen. He was the ultimate morning person, a habit that never died even after retiring from the many years of early rising to catch his commuter train. His first thought was that perhaps she hadn't slept well and rather than loll around awake, she'd join him at his coffee and paper. She quickly dispelled his notion. She was now literally bounding about making no effort to pour her usual starter cup.

"Big doings today, big doings", his wife exclaimed.

The man professed further surprise. He had no recollection of anything unusual planned for the day. Anticipating his ready curiosity, she quickly continued... "It's Macy's, the new Macy's grand opening at ten. Too good to miss. Got to be early in line"

She was almost giddy. There it was. The shopper's supreme siren call…a grand opening. He remembered the last one where she had camped out at two in the morning with a folding chair and poncho to be one of the first hundred to receive a luxury bag of cosmetics at the Mall's new beauty shop.

"If you didn't go, what bonus would you miss this time?" the man asked.

"Ten percent all day. And some crazy specials. Designer jeans at fifty off. Shoes, too. Is this going to be a good day or what", she replied gleefully.

She disappeared into the bathroom before the man had time to ask if she were going alone or with her neighboring best friend.

She always tried to enlist another to help pass the time on long waits. Exiting moments later in bright yellow and pirouetting for him, she was nearly singing, "Channel 3 will be there. Maybe you'll see me on television".

He had to admit she was a dish. She wore her senior years well. If there were some kind of Miss America for seniors, he felt sure she'd make a run of it.

"Don't you have to be first in line for that?" the man asked.

"Not necessarily. Lots of times they look up and down the line and pick someone that stands out", she said.

"Don't you have to wear red for that?"

"Lots think that and there's so much red that nobody in red stands out. The line looks like one big lipstick blur".

"So the yellow".

"And so the yellow".

"I hope you're prepared for disappointment", the man intoned.

"Disappointment? At the Macy's grand opening? It's like another Christmas! I may need to call you to help lug everything home. I'm going to cruise every floor and every aisle till I don't know what day it is. It's going to be a terrific experience."

"Just saying. You know that old adage about experience…"

"What adage?"

"Experience is what you get when you don't get what you expected".

"Don't be so negative. Is this going to be a good day or what?" she again repeated.

His wife began collecting her car keys and purse, suddenly turning as if something had been forgotten. Probably her trusty thermos for a stop at Starbucks, the man thought. But he was wrong. She was still tinkering with appearance.

"Supposing I take my striped boa?", she asked. "No one else is likely to have one in line."

"I don't think it's going to matter", he replied.

"Has something in the paper upset you? You are really doom and gloom today. Might be good if you came with me"

"I can't"

"Why can't you?"

"Because…"

"Because why?"

"Because Macy's grand opening was yesterday".

Rudolph's Little Secret

A few years back, I was asked to participate in a Holiday Pageant for children and, hopefully, bring something new to the affair. Bring something new about Christmas? Whew!

I struggled with the request as so much wonderful, creative stories and songs have been written about the Holiday. But I had always been intrigued and troubled about Rudolph in the sense that we never knew why his nose got that way. Others are troubled as well...Rudolph's author simply lets us believe he came into the world with it. But the Internet has a number of other theories, principally two:

> Rudolph had a parasitic infection in his respiratory system

> Rudolph had an extra dense network of blood vessels in his nose

None of these ideas seemed newsworthy for the pageant. So I invented another one.

## Rudolph's Little Secret

We all know the story of that foggy night
when Santa was faced with a terrible plight.

Grounded he was, with no way to soar
and deliver the gifts he had in store

We all know that Rudolph was hero that night
and saved Santa Claus from his terrible plight.

So end of the story...as far as it goes
But wait! How did he ever get that red nose?

Yes, how in the world did that come about...
That wonderful, glorious, magical snout!

Scientists say they first looked at genes
checking all clues for some in-betweens

Reindeers you know are quite vegetarian
eating anything else is considered barbarian.

Some said his Mom was too fond of the cherry
Others declared that was quite ordinary.

Some said his Dad was addicted to raddish
Too many of those could make your genes baddish

But none of these proved the answer they sought
Try as they might they came up with naught

Yet, there it was for the finding, there to be spied,
the secret that Rudolph so long tried to hide.

See, playing one day with Prancer's cute daughter
A funny thing happened that shouldn't have oughta

She playfully gave him a peck on the cheek
for winning their game of "quick, hide and seek!"

His playmates laughed and pointed their fingers,
he winced as his pride was riddled with stingers.

Being kissed by a girl with everyone staring,
"What could be worse" thought Rudolph despairing

He wished it were he could be laughing instead...
"Oooh, That was awful, I wish I were dead"

Turning crimson, scarlet, ruby, vermillion-
turning every red shade there is by the billion,

his nose came aglow like a great Northern Light
and that way it stayed to everyone's fright.

Dejected, affected he made his way home
attending his gloom, ashamed and alone.

But slowly, slowly he stopped feeling sad
and said to himself "That wasn't so bad".

And each little time he thought of that peck,
His nose would grow redder and redder by heck.

He kept feeling better with each passing day.
He thought of himself in a positive way.

"Someday, yes, some day, I'll have the last laugh.
I'll do something special on Santa's behalf"

Sure as his word his boast did come true
the night of the fog and hero debut

And so ends the story of that special night
when Rudolph's red nose changed darkness to light

And all of it owed to the daughter of Prancer...
Secret no more, the true final answer.

The Truth about UFOs

Faced with a similar request for another pageant, I became struck with the idea of converting the then ongoing rage about Unidentified Flying Objects into a Christmas story.

But UFOs are back in the news again with daily sightings being reported of bizarre nocturnal doings that defy explanation, except for the theory posted here.

# The Truth About UFOs

*The Christmas Connection*

For decades now, the quandary goes on,
From Timbuktu to hither and yon,

That puzzling thing we've seen in the sky,
Maddening us to identify.

Mystic, cryptic, bedeviling us all.
One thing we know, it's not folderal.

What can it be, where is it from?
What does it mean, what's to become?

Troubling us most...is it friend or foe-
This thing we have christened "UFO"?

Some see a globe, some see a thread:
Some say it's white, some say it's red.

Some forewarn it's an alien ship
Some forebode an apocalypse

Some have heard an uncommon tone
Of sounds and words, a babel unknown.

Others avow of a thunderous clap
Rhythmic and clear like rap-a-tap-tap.

Yet all of the experts from "A" to "Z"
So far are baffled on what it can be.

NASA denies that it plays a hand;
Whatever it is, it's not in their plan.

Denial, too, from the CIA,
Suspecting, though, a Copperfield play.

Each of the gurus at MIT,
In unison cry, "Don't ask me!"

Astrologers, too, give it a bye
"Sorry", they say, "We can't edify"

And so it goes on...unsolved, untrumped,
Even Geraldo Rivera is stumped.

But finally now, it all can be told,
the puzzle that so long's been on hold...

Discovery of the easiest kind;
How could we miss it and be so blind?

How could the problem give us such pause?
Cause nobody thought of...Santa Claus!

Yes, Santa Claus!... that was the quirk
Tending his business, doing his work...

From pole to pole and all longitudes,
Thru galaxies, space and all avenues,

Whether Summer, Winter, Spring or Fall,
He's racing about, giving his all

Storing with care each Holiday gift,
So all will be ready on the great 25th.

But what of those witnessed mysteries,
Those shapes, those sounds, those complexities?

Well, the bright light some insist is a ship...
Just the gleam of the sleigh Santa's packed for his trip.

And what of the din some swear they do hear?
Only the prance of Santa's reindeer

And the color red, some have supposed?
Only the glow of ole Rudolph's nose.

And what of those words heard in the night?
Well, those are the words of Santa's delight

Muddled by distance, muffled by flight
Santa declares with all of his might...

Merry Christmas to all everywere!

# About the Author

Talk about two activities of extremes! Stanley Kavan was first a combat bomber pilot surviving 35 hazardous missions over Europe including a very rare single ship, unescorted daylight run earning a Distinguished Flying Cross and later a career recording executive dealing with some of the greatest popular and classical performers ever to grace a musical stage.

A Connecticut native, he commuted for 30 years (and a million miles) to his Columbia Records Manhattan office, then a division of CBS, aiding the careers of Leonard Bernstein, Andre Kostelanetz, Tony Bennett, Johnny Mathis, Doris Day, Barbra Streisand. Simon and Garfunkel and more. His daily 3½ hour rail routine provided a frequent, perfect canvas for his writing hobby. In fact, the clickety clack sound of the trackage inspired one of Mr. Kavan's favorite pieces, The Diamond. His earlier chapbook provided the basis for this all encompassing collection.

Mr. Kavan is a charter, founding member of the National Recording Academy, home of the coveted Grammy awards. Both of his notable professions are suitably covered in two key publications: *Flying Fortress* by Edward Jablonski and *The Label: The Story of Columbia Records* by Gary Marmorstein.